ISBN 978-0-260-97781-6
PIBN 10044391

AMATEUR

YACHTING.

1886.

B. F. ADAMS, PUBLISHER,

112 SOUTH SEVENTH ST.,

PHILADELPHIA.

PREFACE.

The writer hopes this little book will be of interest not only to those who intend to indulge in the healthy, exhilerating sport of yachting but also to those who would like to gain a knowledge of the principles of sailing, through the interest created by the international yacht races.

The directions for sailing and managing a cabin yacht are for beginners, and, as far as possible, such plain words have been used as will enable embryo yachtsmen to follow the directions without confusion, while a short dictionary of technical words has also been added for convenience.

Yachting, besides being beneficial to health, develops the judgment, schools a man into acting promptly in cases of emergency, and increases his self-reliance. It is of benefit not only to the individual, but also to the community.

The National Guard, is useful as a school for drilling our citizens into a body of soldiery, so that in the event of disturbances in our own country or of war with foreign countries we would be able to present a large body of well-drilled men without having in the meantime to support an expensive standing army. England has earned her

supremacy on the sea by the size and power of her navy.
Why should not America increase her power on the sea?
The answer of many is that the United States has within her
borders many acres that want cultivation, many resources
that can be developed. This is true enough, but would it
not be safer for us Americans living near the seacoast to
encourage the development of a taste for aquatic sports, so
that in the event of threatened war by any of the great
powers on the other side of the ocean the Government could
call on thousands of young men to man the ships of a navy
that is slowly but surely increasing, as the Government now
calls on the National Guard in the time of a threatened riot?
These young yachtsmen would not be skilled men-of-
war's men, but they would be vastly superior to men that
have no knowledge of matters aquatic.

Although these few pages treat only of the rudiments
of yachting, the writer has added an outline history of the
representative club of Philadelphia, the Quaker City Yacht
Club, thinking it would be of interest to yachtsmen and
others. Thanks are due to the officers of the club for infor-
mation on this subject, particularly to Asst. Secretary R. W.
Kerswell.

B. F. A.

CONTENTS.

—:—

YACHTS OF THE DELAWARE.

The sloop rig is the favorite with Delaware River yachtsmen for their decked vessels. With the exception of two schooners which have been added to the flotilla of the Quaker City Yacht Club this season the entire fleet of cabin yachts of this club are sloop rigged. The advantages that the sloop has of lying closer to the wind when close hauled and of being handled by a smaller crew are evidently the cause of the preponderance of sloop yachts over others.

Cutter and yawl rigs are seldom seen on the Delaware. The principal difference between a cutter and a sloop is that the former has an adjustable bowsprit, which can be reduced in length by being drawn in on deck during rough weather, thereby decreasing the strain that a long spar causes when the vessel is pitching and rolling in a heavy sea, and also permitting her bows to ride higher so as to more successfully meet the waves when lying to under reduced canvas.

In the yawl-rigged vessel the main boom is so short that the after end clears a small mizzen mast stepped in the extreme stern of the vessel, which carries, as a general rule, a spritsail that extends over the water astern as far or further than does the exceedingly long boom of the sloop or cutter. Although to a novice this rig may appear complicated, it is claimed to be easily handled, as the mizzen sail generally takes care of itself when going about.

A light framework extends beyond the stern. To the end of this a block is attached through which the mizzen sheet is reeved and lead in on deck and belayed to a cleat alongside the steersman, where he can trim the mizzen sail without moving from the helm. By removing the sprit, the lower end of which rests in a grommet attached to the mast and the upper end of which is inserted in another grommet worked in the peak of the mizzen sail, canvas can be reduced very quickly and without even disturbing the halliards of the mainsail. To reduce sail on a sloop is a much more difficult proceeding for two or three men, while to one man it is almost an impossibility when a stiff breeze is blowing.

The yawl rig is very convenient for handling, as preparation can be made for an approaching squall in one or two minutes by one person only, and it is also an excellent rig for rough, rolling weather in the bay or on the ocean, as the leverage and strain on the mast and deck are not near so great as on a vessel with a long main boom.

For these reasons the yawl rig is very suitable for a yacht intended for cruising and which occasionally has to be managed by a small crew. Two men or even a man and a boy can sail such a yacht in comparative safety at sea, but for racing purposes this rig has the same disadvantages that the schooner has in comparison with the sloop and cutter—the sails are too much cut up. While sailing close to the wind this objection is most apparent, for a vessel carrying a large mainsail can be trimmed down closer than can one that has the same number of square feet of canvas divided into two sails.

Yachting, simply as a pleasure and a means of recreation, should be done in a cabin yacht. There is a great deal of excitement in sailing an open boat in a stiff breeze, lying out over the side and holding on by the life lines, but not much comfort, and the drenching and sitting for hours in the wind while acting as living ballast is not very favorable for health. A ballasted cabin yacht of small size is much more suitable for a cruising boat. A centre board sloop yacht of twenty-five feet length is a convenient size for from two to six, and, if sleeping accommodations are not taken in consideration, fifteen or more could be carried. The following directions apply to a yacht of this style and size. A jib and mainsail will be sufficient sail, but if the yacht has a topmast a topsail can be set in addition. Spinnaker, square sail and jib topsail may be omitted as they are of not much practical use on a small sloop during a cruise and only complicate matters for beginners.

The yachts of the Delaware River outside of the Quaker

City Yacht Club are, with a very few exceptions, open boats. The larger ones are decked over for about one-quarter of the length from the bows, about a foot inside of the gunwale along the sides, and two feet or more at the stern; the mast carries a single large sail, gaff and boom, and is stepped close up in the bow and stayed from a short bowsprit forward, and also by side stays that lead to stout timbers which project three or four feet over the water from the deck at the foot of the mast. These are the cat boats, presumably called so from the arrangement of the stays on the above mentioned beams, as timbers somewhat similar and in the same position on large vessels are called catheads. The catheads of a ship are only used in connection with a small tackle to hang the anchors by their rings.

A smaller boat, generally fifteen to seventeen feet long, is the tuckup. This has no cat heads, the mast is set further back, and the beam is not so great as in the cat boat. The decking extends along each gunwale and runs out to the square stern, leaving that portion undecked. The smallest of all are the double-end gunning skiffs, rigged very similar to the tuckups.

All of these boats have centre-boards, those of the cat boats hinged, while the smaller ones lift bodily from the well, and all have immense rudders. Whenever there is a stiff breeze the crew sit up on the decking and gunwale, hold on to the life lines (short pieces of rope fastened securely to the bottom of the boat inside along the well, the free ends having wooden cross handles attached) and then lean backward over the water as the gusts of wind strike the sail, quickly recovering their upright position during the lulls.

The owners of many of the above described boats are organized into two clubs, the Pennsylvania and the Southwark.

The sixth annual regatta of the Pennsylvania Yacht Club came off on May 31, 1886. The start was from Kensington Water Works wharf. The course was to Delanco and return. The race was very quiet at the beginning, but the breeze sprang up shortly after and one of the boats carried away a stay. The first boat in was the William A. Birch; second, the David Bennet; and third, Little Tycoon.

On June 7th, 1886, the twelfth annual regatta of the Southwark Yacht Club occured, Dickinson Street wharf to Chester buoy and return was the course. The Maid was ahead until the buoy was turned when she capsized, and the J. Mitchel came in first. H. D. Boardman was the first boat of the second class, while the Addie was second. The third class was led by the Thomas Ledyard, the Hugh Boyl and Charles Benton following. The J. Nobre, the Joseph Jacobs and the Amanda C., of the fourth class reached home in the order named.

THE QUAKER CITY YACHT CLUB.

In January of the Centennial year a number of gentlemen fond of aquatic sports got together and formed the Philadelphia Yacht Club, with headquarters at 1215 Beach Street, Philadelphia. At the February meeting of the same year the name was changed to Quaker City Yacht Club, and at this meeting the following officers were elected: Commodore, Thomas T. Wills; vice commodore, A. Bancroft; rear commodore, S. Taylor; president, Joseph L. Wills; secretary, C. S. Salin; assistant secretary, Mr. Somers; treasurer, L. B. Boyd.

The following named sloop yachts were enrolled: Samuel Josephs, Phantom, Charles Austin, Kingston, Goddard, W. Tell, Stella, Tacon, Lillie, Ella, Gideon Clarke, Lewes, Columbia, White Wing.

The trustees elected on March 8, 1876, were: Robert Baird, N. B. Boyd, D. W. Murphy and Thomas Robinson; the regatta committee were: John S. Pomeroy, F. Coleman and Albert Dager. The first regatta of the club was held on May 31, 1876, at which four prizes, valued at $60, were awarded. Of the nine yachts that participated the W. Tell came in first and the Coquette second, in the first class, while the Lillie and Stella were first and second in the second class.

About two years after organization the club moved their headquarters to Windmill Island, and shortly after that they removed to New Market and Brown Streets, Philadelphia. In 1882, they made their final move to the Market Street ferry house, Camden, and held their first meeting in the comfortable quarters on November 16 of that year. William Post was then president.

The officers for the present year, 1886, are: Commodore, Charles E. Ellis; vice commodore, Thomas S. Manning; rear commodore, Charles L. Wilson; president, Dr. W. H. Vallette; secretary, W. S. Hoffman; treasurer, S P. Wright; assistant secretary, R. W. Kerswell; measurer, R. G. Wilkins. Board of Trustees—H. D. Walls, R. P. Thompson, S. A. Wood, T. S. Manning. Regatta Committee—H. Clay Funk, W. J. Walker, E. A. Hildebrand, R. M. Fitch, Jr., Oswald McAllister and S. P. Wright.

Every year since the organization of the club a regatta has been held at the opening of the yachting season, about the first of June, and the prizes for the winning yachts have increased in beauty and value, those for the Eleventh Annual Regatta being:

Schooner class—Fine nickle plated clock.

First class sloops—For the first a taffrail log, and for the second a swinging ice pitcher and goblet.

Second class sloops—Binnacle and compass.

Third class sloops—The first a champion flag; second, American yacht ensign, and third, a cabin light.

Fifth class—A champion flag. There were no fourth class entries. The above are the regular club prizes, while a number of handsome special prizes were given by several members of the club. These were:

The Charles D. Middleton Challenge Cup, for first class sloops, won by Venitzia, this is of solid silver.

The Commodore Charies E. Ellis Challenge Cup, solid silver, for the yacht making fastest time ever made over the course, won by Venitzia.

The Commodore W. H. Vallette Challenge Cup, for second class sloops, won by Consort, solid silver.

All of the above prizes are of solid silver and are very handsome. Each of them have to be won three times in succession to be held perpetually by the winner.

GETTING UNDER WAY.

On the young yachtsman's first attempt to manage a sloop he should have a companion to assist. We will suppose the vessel to be anchored at some distance from other vessels, so there will be no danger of collision through inexperience. If the yacht is anchored in a moderately strong tide-way and there is delay in getting headway after the anchor is loosened, she is in danger of drifting into other vessels or wharves, or of running ashore, unless the attempt is made during slack water, or at the change of tide—of the two changes of tide that from high to low is the best, for then the water is deepest and there is less danger of running aground. A moderate breeze off shore and flood tide just finished make

CLOVE HITCH.

the best combination of circumstances to get successfully under way. After rowing to the yacht, the painter, or rope attached to the bow of the skiff, should be made fast to a ringbolt or cleat, which, as a rule, is bolted to the deck aft of the rudder post. The yachtsman should not make a clumsy knot, but should fasten the painter by making a clove hitch.

15

If the sloop has been left in order the mainsail will be found neatly tied down to the boom by canvas strips, or sail stops, and the boom supported near its after end by a truss. The truss should be removed by lifting the boom, when that spar will be supported by the topping lift, or the rope leading from the masthead to the end of the boom. The sail stops should next be untied and placed with the truss and other loose articles in the cabin, as the cockpit should be kept clear, to prevent the sheet from fouling. If the yacht is not provided with a steering wheel, the tiller, or handle for the rudder, should be gotten from the cabin and inserted in the mortice in the rudder-head. While one is doing this his companion can be casting loose the jib, which is generally tied down not by removable sail stops, but by short pieces of thick twine or marlin, fastened at one end with small staples in pairs on each side of the bowsprit. They are tied over the sail when it is lowered, but when loosened hang on both sides of the bowsprit. If these are untied carefully the jib will lie in a flat roll, without falling overboard.

If the jib sheets are led aft to the cockpit for convenience of working, the ends should be slightly fastened to their respective cleats. The main sheet should be neatly coiled in the centre of the cockpit floor, commencing the coil not from the free end, but from the part nearest to the boom, and the coil turned over so as to allow it to run free. This rope is quite long and is apt to get tangled, which may cause a capsize. It is a bad plan to make fast to a cleat the main sheet of a small yacht.

While waiting for a breeze the young yachtsman is apt to make the sheets fast, abandon the helm and seek shelter from a scorching sun under shadow of the sails, or, perhaps, in the cabin. Even while undergoing the annoyance and discomfort of being broiled in the sun he had better keep one hand on the tiller and the other on the free end of the main sheet, as a sudden gust may capsize the

BOWSPRIT AND JIB.

boat if an unballasted one, or even one that is lightly ballasted, as small light-draft cabin yachts usually are.

As the yacht in the present instance is supposed to be some distance from other vessels the anchor can be raised before the mainsail is hoisted, but the best plan generally, and the only one when she is surrounded by a fleet, of other yachts, or when the wind is blowing on shore, is to make sail and then weigh anchor. Not only is this form of getting under way frequently necessary, but it is most yachtsmanlike. The proceedings are as follows: If the yacht is simply anchored and riding with a long chain or cable, this should be shortened by hauling in until she is directly over the anchor. To fasten the chain at that length, three or four turns should be given around the knighthead, the last or topmost crossing under the one below it, as represented in the cut. If she is riding at moorings the chain is cast off from the yacht and remains supported by a buoy until the yacht's return.

Sail should be hoisted after shortening the chain, first the mainsail by the throat and peak halliards; then the jib by means of the jib halliard, making it secure to its proper cleat, but leaving the sheets loose. The throat halliard, which is most instrumental in hoisting the mainsail, is attached to the gaff at the throat, that is the part nearest

KNIGHTHEAD. the mast, and, after being reeved through blocks both on gaff and masthead, passes down along the port side of the mast and is fastened to a cleat on that side, or, what is better in a small yacht, it is led back over the trunk by passing through a small brass pulley screwed to the deck, to the cockpit, where the slack can be taken in and where it is belayed to a cleat on the port side of the trunk.

The peak halliard, which is to raise the outer end or peak of the mainsail and make the sail lie as flat as possible, is fastened to a cleat in a corresponding position on the starboard side, and the slack of this must be taken in at the same time as is that of the throat halliard, but not so rapidly as to raise the peak of the gaff above the level of the throat, as by so doing the gaff is apt to become jammed.

Remember, *the mainsheet should be perfectly loose* while this is being done, so that the boom may swing in the direction of the wind and the sail offer no resistance to it. The throat halliard should be drawn so tight that the boom will just clear the saddle, which surrounds the mast and which will support the boom after sailing for a short time, as the sail and halliards will stretch. Then the peak may be drawn up to its proper position.

Now you are ready to weigh anchor. This can be done by one person if the anchorage ground is soft mud, but if it is stiff clay or gravel and the flukes of the anchor are broad, it may take the strength of two to break anchorage without a windlass. If a few feet of chain are paid out quickly the chain will be loose enough to throw over a small iron pulley that is attached to the side of the bowsprit on many small yachts two or three feet from the bows and which gives a purchase in hauling on the chain. Then by the application of the strength of the crew the flukes can be drawn out. As soon as the anchor comes away one of the yachtsmen may draw it up as rapidly as convenient while the other quickly regains the helm.

Once the anchor is clear of the river bottom the yacht will drift, and the sooner headway is obtained the better, as

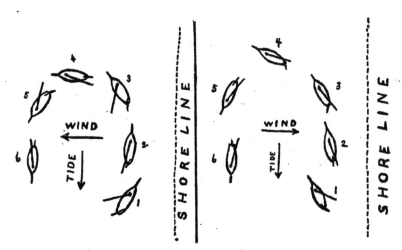

CASTING THE YACHT'S HEAD.

the rudder has no command over the boat until she moves forward.

As the yacht has been anchored at the head her stern will swing off from the wind, inclining in the direction of the expiring tide, which position is represented in the left-hand diagram at figure 1.

To make her head fall off the wind, draw the weather jib sheet taut and put the helm hard up, that is move the tiller in the direction from which the wind is blowing. The breeze filling the jib, will push the yacht's head around and give her a slight forward motion. Next trim in the main sheet, drawing the boom almost in a line with the keel. Now the full pressure of the wind will be on the sails, and as the vessel gains headway her rudder will act, throwing her head still further from the wind. As the wind draws across the beam, (position No. 2) loosen the main sheet and let the boom swing out to prevent it from gybing as the yacht moves to position No. 3. (Gybing occurs when the wind, *coming over the stern,* shifts, and catches the sails on the side opposite to that which it was originally, swinging the boom over rapidly, and is attended by more or less danger. To prevent gybing a light line or boom guy is attached to the boom near the sheet block and lead forward to the leeward mainstay). Then bring the helm amidships or in a line with the keel, rapidly draw in the main sheet again until the boom approaches a line parallel with the direction of the wind, put the helm in the same position as at first and look out for your head—keep clear of the sheet. The wind will catch the sail on the opposite side and cause the boom to swing over with a rapidity in proportion to the strength of the breeze. This mode of turning the yacht so as to bring the wind on the opposite side over the stern is termed wearing and should be done only with reduced sail, unless the breeze is very moderate. In heavy weather it is attended with considerable danger.

Remember to have the main sheet clear before this move is made as the boom swings with great force and should be brought up gradually, to prevent the carrying away of blocks. It is very probable you will have the skin scraped from your hands on the first attempt to wear.

If you should be so unfortunate as to have the blocks

torn from the boom during this movement, still hold the helm in the same position and *cast loose the jib sheets* before headway is lost, when the yacht will keep right on in a circle, until she heads the wind. After arriving at this position the helm should be brought in a line with the keel again. Now the disabled boom will be overdeck, when sail can be lowered and repairs made, anchoring first if still near the shore or if in danger of drifting into other vessels.

After everything is put in order another attempt should be made, and the same proceedings gone through with as before. After arriving at position No. 6, the yacht heading on her intended course, the helm should be brought amidships. As you intend sailing with the wind on the beam, the centre-board should be lowered to diminish lee-way, or drifting sideways before the wind. If the centre-board does not run out freely, luff the yacht, in other words run her head on the wind, when the pressure will be taken from the board and it will slip out readily. Trim down first the main sheet, and as you do so the helm may be put up slightly as the pressure of the wind will be all on the mainsail, which, as it is abaft the mast, will give the boat a tendency to run up into the wind, which effort the helm put up a trifle will counteract. Now draw taut the lee jib sheet, and make the jib lie almost flat. As the jib is trimmed down the helm can be brought to the amidships position, or very near to it. In a yacht the sails of which are well balanced the rudder will be almost in a line with the keel.

Should the wind at the time of starting blow on shore, instead of off, getting under way will be more difficult. Still if the yachtsman has acquired a little experience in starting under more favorable circumstances he may make the attempt with an on-shore wind with good chances of success.

The yacht should be anchored far enough from the shore to insure a floating depth of water at least three of her lengths from her stern, which in this case will be nearest the shore, inclining, as before, in the direction of the tide. The space between the yacht and shore, or rather limit of floating depth, is necessary, as before headway can be made the wind will cause the yacht to drift sideways. Although an expert yachtsman can get under way with very little lee-room, probably with less than a single vessel's length of space, it will be necessary for a beginner to give himself more room or stand a very great chance of being driven hard ashore, which at high water would compel him to give up the sail for that day, or that tide, at least.

The best stage of the tide when getting under way with the wind off-shore is at slack water or the turn of the tide, but with the wind on-shore the best time is while the tide is flowing, provided there are no other vessels near to drift into. The tide flowing will cause the yacht to lie more or less parallel with the shore and broadside to the inblowing breeze. In this position her jib will fill more readily, and, as her head falls away before the breeze, the mainsheet can be trimmed in and headway can be made before the drift sideways on shore has become very great. The slightest headway gives control through the rudder and if the helm is gently put down the yacht will gradually incline off shore.

When the yacht arrives at figure 4, in the right hand diagram, she is close hauled on the port tack. By loosening the jib sheet, keeping the helm to starboard and trimming in the mainsheet she will gradually come head to the wind, and a little later will have the wind on the starboard, as in figure 5, when the lee jib sheet should be hauled taut, and the main sheet be brought home so that the sail will draw.

Tacking, this mode of bringing the wind on the other side of the sail, is preferable to wearing and is always the safest. When the wind is on the starboard side the vessel is on the starboard tack, when the wind is on the port side the vessel is on the port tack. By sailing first on one tack then on the other, vessels proceed in the direction from which the wind is blowing. A fore-and-aft vessel will sail closer to the wind than will a square rigged one, and the flatter the sails lie the closer to the wind can the vessel be brought. The jib or staysail is sometimes laced to a boom to diminish its curving so that it will draw more than it would otherwise.

REDUCING SAIL.

Always keep a sharp lookout to windward for squalls, which are frequently quite severe. On a clear summer day they generally accompany a black mass of clouds, sometimes with thunder and lightning, which notify their approach, followed by a heavy rainfall. On cloudy days as a rule they come up without any meteorological phenomena other than those prevailing at the time.

Watch the small vessels to windward of you. If they reduce sail it is time for you also to take in sail. Don't delay, for a squall travels swiftly and will be on you before you are ready for it if sail is not taken in rapidly. If the water a hundred yards or so to windward shows ripples be ready to meet the gust with the helm. Keep jib sheets clear. The writer has been caught in a heavy blow when the jib sheets had got jammed in the cleat to which they were belayed. The wind pressed the yacht so far over that although the helm was put hard down she would not come up into the wind, from the fact that owing to the excessive heeling over only a small portion of the rudder was immersed. If the wind could have been spilled from the jib all would have been well. The rain fell in torrents, the wind roared and the water washed into the cockpit. The boom and lower part of the mainsail dragging in the water further counter-acted the diminished force of the rudder and also assisted in throwing her over. The yacht would have capsized in a very short time and foundered, as she was ballasted suffici-ently to cause that catastrophe. Leaving the helm to take care of itself and rushing forward the jib halliards were loosened and by violently pulling on the jib downhaul the jib was taken in, and by again forcing down the helm she slowly came around, head to the wind, and sail was reduced.

No damage was done at the time, further than loosing overboard all the loose articles that were on deck. The rainfall was so dense that it was some time before all the articles that did not sink could be found and picked up.

This was a very narrow escape and impressed on us the wisdom of keeping all running rigging in order. The squall, as they usually are, was as short lived as it was severe and in half an hour after our heeling over the sun was shining brightly and drying our clothing, a gentle breeze blowing, the thunder dying away and the black cloud disappearing in the Northeast.

Reducing sail should be practiced as soon as possible and thereby the young yachtsman will be prepared and know how to act in case of a blow.

If you wish to take in sail while tacking or sailing with the wind on the beam put down the helm and trim in the mainsheet, which action will throw the yacht's head to the wind, and relieve the sails of pressure. Lower the peak, then the throat, by loosening the corresponding halliards and pulling on the downhaul, or rope attached to the jaws of the gaff and running alongside the mast to the deck. Lower the sail sufficiently to allow whichever row of reef points you wish to fasten to be passed around and tied beneath the boom.

The reef points are short pieces of cordage arranged in two or more rows across the sail; the lowest row, or first reef, being near the foot. Each point passes through the sail and is knotted and

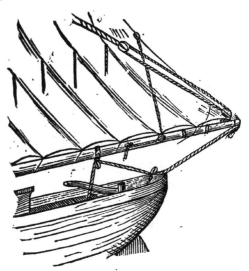

BOOM AND MAINSAIL.

secured in position, an end hanging down on each side of the sail far enough to admit of being tied beneath the boom when the sail is lowered sufficiently. They should always be tied with reef knots. On the back edge of the sail, or what is technically known as the leech, at the end of each row of reef points is worked in the bolt rope of the canvas a loop of rope, or reef cringle, containing a small iron ring. One end of a short piece of rope, called a reef pennant, is attached to one side of the boom beneath the reef cringles, the other end is passed up and through the reef cringle of whichever reef is intended to be put in the sail, down on the other side and through a block screwed to the side of the boom, and, is led from thence forward to a cleat on the underside of the boom, to which it is belayed.

As the halliards are loosened the leech of the sail is drawn down by means of the reef pennant and is kept in position by belaying the pennant to the cleat, which is placed far enough inboard to be reached conveniently from the deck. Rings corresponding to the reef cringles are also fastened to the sail at the end of each row of reef points nearest the mast. This portion of the sail is called the luff and the rings are termed luff cringles.

The halliards should be made fast temporarily and one of you should commence tying the reef points nearest the mast, first passing a short piece of rope through the luff cringle and tying beneath the boom, working aft, while the steersman can tie those nearest to him and at the same time tend the tiller.

If the yacht looses headway and falls off before the wind, after several points are tied the halliards can be drawn up temporarily, the sheet trimmed in, and, after headway is gained, the yacht can again be thrown up in the wind, when the halliards can be loosened and the tying of the remaining points finished.

If care is taken to cast loose the jib sheets before this manoeuvre is executed the chances are very small of the yacht's falling away before the wind until the reefing is finished, while, on the contrary, if the jib is full of wind when the mainsail halliards are lowered it may be almost impossible to keep the yacht in the wind's eye with the rudder, particularly if she carries a very large jib.

After the tying is finished the halliards should be drawn tight and made fast, when the yacht can be allowed to fall away upon her course again.

A reefed mainsail will not lie as smooth and flat as one that is hoisted to its full height, therefore the yacht can not run as close to the wind as before. Have the luff well tied down, as that portion of the sail if loose or baggy will shake before it would if properly tied. The shaking signifies that the wind is not pressing against the sail to the greatest advantage and warns the steersman to put up his helm slightly so the yacht will drop off a trifle.

REEF KNOT.

In tying the points care should be taken to make reef knots, like this shown in the accompanying cut, as they can be untied with comparative ease, and will not work loose as will be the case with a knot made by passing the ends of the cord in the opposite direction in making the second or upper portion of the knot. Sailors call the latter a granny's knot.

Sail stops should be tied with reef knots, and this knot should be made in almost all temporary ties where two ends of a cord or rope are fastened together. If made properly it will not slip, no matter how much strain is put on the rope.

When sailing with a freshening wind abaft the beam and wishing to reduce sail the precaution should be taken to drop the peak of the mainsail before bringing the yacht around into the wind. It is also wise to hoist the end of the boom with the topping lift, by means of the topping lift tackle. While sailing large the breeze may increase very much without being noticed, so that due caution should be observed before bringing the wind on the beam in the attempt to head the yacht to the wind.

After dropping the peak and loosening the jib sheets, put down the helm, and, if the breeze is very strong, let the main sheet run out as far as it will, so as to spill as much of the wind as possible. If she obeys her helm readily she will swing around and quickly pass the danger point of the movement, which is when the wind is on the beam. As her head comes up in the wind trim in the mainsheet rapidly and give her good headway before running up into the wind, after which the reefing can be done, as described above. Unless you are in very rough water you will get around safely.

If the wind increases and you put a second reef in the mainsail you will have difficulty in keeping the yacht's head to the wind, as the entire jib will be too much head sail for the reduced mainsail. The jibs on large vessels have an extra piece hooked or laced to the bottom part, called the bonnet. By taking out the bonnet the sail is reduced. The easiest plan to reduce a small yacht's jib is to lower it two or three feet and tie up the foot by means of a row of reef points.

While sailing in the bay, if you should be caught in a hard gale, when the tops of the waves are chopped off and sent through the air in spinning drops, and you think that it will not be safe to attempt to ride out the storm, you had better scud before the wind, unless by doing so you would be approaching a lee shore.

Scudding under the close reefed mainsail is not safe for several reasons: First, the weight of the boom will cause the yacht to roll and strain the mast, and through it the deck; second, if the wind is gusty and shifts through several points, there is great danger of gybing, which, at such a time, would be almost certain to break the boom or carry something away, thereby incurring great danger of foundering.

A storm trysail should be set for scudding. Luff the yacht and take in altogether the mainsail. Keep the yacht's head to wind under the jib alone by putting the helm down and tending jib sheet after the mainsail is lowered; do not let her fall broadside to the waves, but spill the wind from the jib by loosening the lee jib sheet, the other to be entirely loose; she may be able to run before the wind under jib alone, but it is safest to get storm trysail hoisted before coming around. Truss the boom and lash down; unhook mainsheet from boom; unhook peak halliards from gaff; bring out trysail and lace the forward edge, or luff, to the mast, attaching the peak halliards to the head, and the mainsheet to the clew, or outer lower corner; hoist away and trim in sheet. Watch for a lull and wear and you will be scudding under a storm trysail and jib. The jib may now be taken in to reduce strain on the mast.

The danger in scudding lies in the chance of waves overtaking the yacht and pouring in over the stern. If you are in water that is not too deep and you have a good anchor and chain it is preferable to ride at anchor with a long chain.

Carrying away the sails or breaking the mast, when anchoring is not available, is a misfortune which can be met by rigging a sea anchor, in this manner: Lash three spars, oars, boathooks, or anything that is handy into a triangle; fasten securely across this frame a spare sail and in the middle of one of the spars fasten a heavy weight, a spare anchor or piece of ballast; to each of the sides of the triangle securely fasten a short piece of rope, as long as one side of the triangle, and tie their free ends together; fasten your cable or chain to this and throw overboard and fasten at the bow. This will hold her head to the wind and slightly break the force of the waves.

SAILING AT NIGHT.

A sailing vessel while in motion has a green lantern fixed on her starboard bow and so protected by boxing that the rays from it are cast directly ahead and from thence through a section of a circle slightly abaft the starboard beam. On the port side a red lantern is fixed in a corresponding manner so that its light is seen only on the port side of the vessel within the prescribed limit.

On small vessels, especially in rough weather, such lights with their screens are difficult to attach, and as substitutes for them a green and a red lantern can be placed in a bucket or an empty box on deck so as to be unseen until the approach of a vessel, when the proper lantern can be lifted from the box and shown on the side toward the approaching danger, the light to be carefully screened from the other side and the stern of the yacht by the body of the person showing it. This arrangement will answer very well where only occasional voyages are made by night, but care must be taken not to show the wrong light. *The green to be shown on the starboard or right hand side, the red on the port or left hand side.*

The colored lights are not to be used while at anchor; but a white light is to be hung to the fore stay six or eight feet above the deck, unprotected, so as to show all around the horizon. This light must be removed when getting under way again, for to sail with it would very likely be the cause of a collision, as showing the white light in connection with the colored ones implies the vessel to be a steamer, and therefore restricts the vessel's right of way. The white light can be temporarily shown from the stern on the approach of a vessel from that direction.

The danger of being run down or of running down something else is very much increased in the neighborhood of cities, where many vessels are passing and repassing continually. This risk is even greater at night than during the day as the young sailor is apt to become confused by the multiplicity of lights; for this reason a sharp lookout should be kept, especially for ferry boats, which can be recognized by their two white lights—one on each end, together with the colored side lights. Other steam vessels ordinarily carry a single white light besides the colored lights.

Two white lights, one above the other, together with the side lights denote a tug or steamer towing another vessel. To attempt to cross the stern of a vessel with lights arranged in this manner would bring the yachtsman to grief through the intervention of the towing hawser and the vessel being towed, which also carries side lights, minus the white if she is a sailing vessel.

If either a sailing or steam vessel is not under control or is engaged in dredging or laying telegraph cables she exhibits three red lights hanging in a row one over the other.

These are the only arrangements of lights likely to be met with on the Delaware. There are several other combinations used by pilots and by fishermen, where numbers congregate, which signify that the vessels are engaged in trawling, fishing with drift net, etc., but which if mentioned here would be apt only to confuse the reader.

Now a few rules concerning the direction of steering when meeting or crossing lights:

If *both the red and green lights* of a vessel are seen at once *directly ahead* (figure 2) put your helm to port, unless you are on the starboard tack (figure 1), in which case you have the right of way. If you are close hauled on the starboard tack and the vessel continues to bear down on you, do not attempt to put up your helm and fall off to port; keep cool; probably her steersman may not have seen you in the darkness; shout to him to port his helm. Then, at the last moment, you must decide whether to put yours to port or not, as by doing so your yacht will be placed broadside to the approaching vessel and headway will be lost.

If you wish to pass to the left, contrary to the rule, you must turn the yacht's head to port while a considerable distance away, showing your green light, thereby signifying your intention to the steersman of the other vessel that you intend to pass him on that side. If this move is

DIAGRAM ILLUSTRATING STEERING RULES.

understood the red light of the other vessel will disappear
and only the green will be visible, when the vessels will be
in safe relative positions.

In the first of the above cases to pass each other your
red light must oppose his; in the second case your green
light must oppose his.

There is doubt and danger only when a green is op-
posed to a red, or a red to a green. A green light ahead on
your red light or port side signifies that a vessel is sailing
on a line that will cross your bow (3 and 4), or, if she is a
considerable distance to the port, you stand a greater chance
of crossing her bow. In this case watch her carefully.
If you are on the starboard tack (figure 1) you have the
right of way and can hold your course. If she is coming

on a diagonal line to meet you, you know she is on the port tack and must give away to you.

If she is going in the same general direction as you are and on the starboard tack (figure 4) you will either have to luff or fall away if there is danger of collision because your vessel is *to the windward.*

The above rules embrace those for steering by daylight. In a few words they are as follows:

A vessel sailing free meeting a vessel tacking must give way so as allow the vessel sailing close to pass without falling off from the wind or luffing. All the vessels on the right of the dotted line are sailing free and should give way to 1, 3 and 4. The parallel lines in the diagram represent the direction of the wind. The boom always swings over the leeward side of the yacht.

When two vessels meet while tacking (as in 4 and 3) the one having the wind on the starboard bow, or, in other words, the one on the starboard tack, has the right of way.

If both of the meeting vessels are sailing free with the wind on the same side (as in 2 and 7, or 5 and 6) the windward vessel must give way to the other; if both are running free with the wind on different sides (figures 5 and 2) the one with the wind on the starboard side of the sail has the right of way.

A vessel with the wind aft and with her boom carried to starboard must keep out of the way of all others (figure 7).

These rules will govern the yachtsman's actions when meeting sailing vessels; with steamers they can be followed in a modified way; as steamers are under much better control than vessels that move through the medium of wind pressure, they are supposed to give up the right of way. By using discretion and partly following the same rules when meeting steamers very little risk of collision will be run.

When steamers pass each other to the left they signify their intention of doing so by *two* short whistles, when passing to the right they blow only one whistle.

ANCHORING.

As the anchor is drawn up at the time of getting under way the mud should be washed from it and the chain, and it should be hung by one fluke over the gunwale, or fished, where it will not be in the way of the jib sheets when going about.

The chain should, remain on deck after weighing anchor long enough to become dry, and then be run, down through the chain hole in the deck. Have its inner end securely fastened to a ringbolt, around a beam, or to the foot of the mast, to prevent it from being lost overboard when anchoring in deep water. Do not depend on this fastening to ride at anchor with, but give two or three turns around the knighthead or a stanchion on deck.

When about to anchor, throw the yacht's head up in the wind, take in the jib, and, after headway is checked, let go the anchor, at the same time haul down the mainsail. Be care-ful to let the anchor go down crown first and see that the chain does not wrap around either the shank or the flukes, as a fouled anchor will not hold to the bottom. Let out plenty of chain if there is a hard bottom and the current or tide is strong, as the yacht may drag her anchor. This can be discovered by placing your hand on the chain, when if dragging a jarring or quivering motion will be felt. In that case let out more chain, the full length if necessary. If she still drags, draw up the anchor to see that it is not fouled.

If running before the wind to the anchorage, and you are unable to come about, take in mainsail when a considerable distance from the place selected and run up to it under the jib alone. As the yacht's speed decreases you can judge at what distance to take in the jib. If running against a strong tide with a light wind the sails can be carried longer than when the tide is running with you.

Make allowance both for the length of chain to be run out and the drift or dragging of the anchor before it takes hold, also take into consideration the direction of tide and wind, particularly the former. If anchoring near other vessels make allowance for the tide's swinging the vessel around, so that you will neither foul chains nor collide.

Frequently· while sailing on the river with a light breeze you will find it to advantage to anchor when the tide turns in the direction opposite to your course. A square-sail can easily be converted into an awning at such times by unhooking the peak halliards, after the mainsail is furled and trussed, and stretching the square-sail along the top of the gaff and boom, the spars used as yards being at right angles with the boom, one near the throat the other over the stern sheets, and fastened. The throat halliards should be drawn so as to raise the boom about two feet from its usual position on the saddle, then the sides of the awning may be tied by pieces of marlin to small rings or staples fastened in the deck near the gunwale. These will prevent the light breeze from tipping up the awning on either side. See that you get the awning cleared away in time for a blow, if one should come up, or you will be very likely to lose it.

An awning of some sort, if nothing better than light muslin, should be carried, as there will be many hours of anchoring during midday in a hot sun and waiting for the tide to turn or a breeze to spring up, and shelter on deck at such a time will be found very acceptable, as the cabin will be then extremely close.

During these anchorages the yachtsmen wile away their time by playing games, telling stories, reading, and, to those who are so inclined, a quiet smoke and meditation followed by a refreshing nap is then indulged in. Several men crowded into a small cabin could not have near the comfort and actual pleasure that they would have on deck, getting the benefit of the little catspaws that occasionally ripple the surface of the water.

At the turn of tide or the appearance of an increasing breeze, throw the books and papers into the cabin, put away the games, wake the slumberers, clear away the awning, hoist sail and up with the anchor, when away you go, dashing through the water and heading for your next anchorage.

When anchoring for the night run up a creek or into a

cove off from the channel as then you will not be run down, even if your white light blows out as it is very apt to on gusty nights.

At the mouth of almost every creek there is a sandbar, frequently so high that it is exposed at low tide, while just within there is deep water, in some instances twenty feet or more. This should be remembered when approaching a strange creek and due precaution should be taken. It is best to reduce sail and draw up the centreboard, half way, at least, when the wind is on the beam.

A long oar or boathook is useful for sounding when in ten feet of water or less; for a greater depth than that a short lead-line can be used.

A creek frequently has a channel of considerable depth through its bar, but seldom is it in a direct line with its mouth; it is more apt to be some distance below, sometimes half a mile. A good chart will enable you to get in with less trouble than any attempt to search for the channel without one will, but with a little care a yacht drawing three or four feet of water can be gotten safely within a creek by using the small boat to search for the position of the channel.

Do not anchor in very shallow water, especially if the tide is high. The height of the tide, the draft of the yacht and at least three feet additional should be allowed in quiet water. Say, for instance, it is high water when you wish to anchor. The regular tides on the Delaware are between five and six feet in height, add to six feet your draft, say three feet, and also three feet more; these sums amount to twelve feet. If there is a swell at least two feet more should be added. By anchoring in less water than this the yacht may settle on the anchor and break her planking. If you can awaken at the turn of the tide you had better attend to the chain, as the yacht's swinging around is apt to foul the anchor, although this risk can be diminished by mooring or by anchoring short, say with a length of chain double the depth of water, or less. This length will not allow the anchor to hold in a blow.

Mooring in the simplest manner is done by letting out considerable chain—twice as much as you intend to ride at —and then dropping another anchor. The chain attached to the first anchor can be drawn in as the other is paid out, until one-half is drawn in and the vessel is an equal distance from each. This will prevent swinging with the tide, and the holding is also more secure during a blow. The centre board should be drawn up and fastened before anchoring.

For a light draft cabin yacht twenty-five feet long an anchor weighing sixty or seventy-five pounds will be sufficiently heavy. Chain is far superior to rope for anchoring. It takes up less room, is stronger, can be kept cleaner, and its extra weight will cause the anchor to hold better. A suitable size is 5·16 inch, measuring the diameter of the iron. It will take a strain of three tons to break a chain of this size, while it weighs less than a pound to the foot. Rope strong enough to stand this strain would have to be $3\frac{1}{2}$ inches in circumference. Rope is always measured around; a three inch rope being nearly one inch in diameter, as the circumference is a fraction over three times the diameter. A rope of this size has a working strength of about one and one-half tons.

If it is necessary to fasten a rope to a spare anchor a rolling hitch should be made, which is a combination of a round turn and a clove hitch. The round turn is made by passing the end twice through the ring instead of once as is represented in the cut on page 15 after which the clove hitch is made and the end of the rope is seized to the standing part. The seizing is done by wrapping small stuff, such as rope yarn, eight or ten times around both the end and the part it lies on and tying tight, thus making it secure.

A convenient length of chain for anchoring a small yacht is one hundred feet, although sixty feet will do as with that length you can anchor quite securely in twenty feet of water.

The channel in the Delaware varies from twenty-five to fifty feet in depth, and some places in the bay it is sixty feet deep. Probably the deepest place this side of Fort Delaware is near the foot of Chestnut Street, Philadelphia, where there are fifty-eight feet of water.

If your anchor should become fast on the bottom, by catching in sunken wreckage, or masses of rock, it can be liberated by rowing in the small boat over the spot where it lies and at the same time dragging the bight or loop of a rope weighted so that it will catch across the upper fluke, then by rowing and pulling on the rope the anchor may be loosened sufficiently to be drawn up from the deck of the yacht. If it is securely fastened and the rope slips off, catch it again and pass a small iron ring over both ends of the rope, then by shaking it will run down to the anchor and lock the loop or bight securely around the fluke, when by passing the ends aboard the yacht and giving them a turn around the windlass, or even by heaving with main strength, the anchor may be drawn to the deck, crown uppermost.

If you intend anchoring where it is probable the anchor will be caught make the end of the rope or chain fast to the crown and then seize it at two or three feet from the end to the ring by one or two pieces of twine or rope yarn. When stuck, by winding it on the windlass the rope yarn will break and allow the anchor to be drawn out by the crown.

When the inner end of the anchor chain or rope slips overboard it can be got by rowing with a grapnell across its length. With rope to be dragged for, three large fish hooks can be bound back to back and used as a grapnell. They will readily catch in the strands.

THE YACHT'S TENDER.

A strong and light tender for the yacht is a very necessary adjunct. It should be short, broad and shallow. The
first quality will enable it to be stowed and lashed, bottom
up, on the trunk when necessary in rough weather, breadth
will give it buoyancy, stability, and also room for the occu-
pants, while shallowness will allow it to be rowed close to a
flat shore or over a bar, and will enable it to be towed easily
after the yacht; the last quality will also permit it to be
stowed on the trunk handier, as the boom can be made to
clear it by lifting its end with the topping lift in a less
degree than would be necessary with a deeper boat.

Another point in favor of a shallow boat is that short
oars can be used, and, therefore, there will be less exertion
in rowing. The oars should not be broad, but with a
moderately long blade. They will remain in good order
much longer if bound near the end of the blade with tin or
sheet iron, or, what is better, copper.

Clinker-built double-end gunning skiffs (with the lower
edge of each strake or plank overlapping the one next
beneath, in the same manner as do the weatherboards of a

frame house) combine the qualities of strength and lightness in a great degree. The only objection to these boats is when injured they are difficult to repair.

Although the ordinary carvel-built boats (those with the edges of the stakes joining) are somewhat heavier, they will stand rougher usage, and if the planking should be broken they can be temporarily repaired by tacking a piece of sheet lead, or even canvas over the damaged parts. The rough, clinker-built boats cannot be repaired in this manner very successfully.

There is also built a hoop-fastened boat, which has very little framework. The boards are joined edge to edge as in the ordinary carvel and are held together by iron hoops passing around outside the planking, each hoop ending in a round rod which has a thread cut in it on which a nut is screwed after the rod passes through the gunwale and a small iron plate. This is also lighter than the ordinary boat.

The painter should be securely fastened in the bow and be at least fifteen feet long. When making fast to a wharf either at high or at low tide with the intention of leaving the boat for several hours be sure to give plenty of rope, or the bow will be suspended if the tide falls and the stern will sink, filling her, while if the tide rises the bow will be held down and she will be filled in that manner.

When making fast to a wharf where there is a strong tideway she will be prevented from swinging around with

the turn of the tide, and becoming damaged, by anchoring
her at the stern with a kedge or small anchor. The latter,
although convenient, is not a necessary article in a boat's
outfit, but a leather bailer or scoop with wooden handle
should always be in the boat. A boathook is also useful.
Rowlocks should be fastened with twine or marlin.

When rowing through a swell caused by a steamboat
keep the boat's head to the waves. Attempting to make fast
to a vessel in motion is dangerous. When doing so the
head of the rowboat should be in the same direction as the
moving vessel, and as soon as the end of the painter is passed
on board no time should be lost in going to the stern of the
boat and sitting down, as a light boat towed rapidly through
the water with a weight near the bow is almost sure to
plunge under bow first and turn over.

A leaky boat can be emptied of water when the yacht is
sailing rapidly by tying her short, so as to slightly lift her head
out of water. If she leakes near the stern nearly all of the
water will pass out, and this will save a great deal of work
bailing. As a rule boats in tow should be tied short. An
exception is when running before the wind in a stiff breeze.

In getting into a small boat from the water climb over the
the stern, as an attempt to get in over the side will capsize her.

A ringbolt should be securely fastened in the stern as
well as in the bow. The stern ringbolt is useful in getting
her on deck, in mooring her to prevent her from swinging
with the tide, and of most importance in towing the yacht

when necessary. By placing heavy weights in the stern of the rowboat, the labor of towing will be much diminished.

When landing on a shore or beach it is well to pull up the boat and make the painter fast to the kedge if you have one, and bury one fluke in the sand, to prevent the rising tide from floating her off. If the boat is heavy, the tide is falling and you wish to keep her afloat, push her back into water two or three feet deep and anchor her with the kedge, then wade ashore.

A light, shallow boat such as has been suggested for a yacht's tender is intended only for rowing. On account of light draft and no centre board even if supplied with a small sail she could only run before the wind. Still it is possible to work to windward with such a boat by using lee-boards. The fishermen on the seacoast use these boards in sailing over the sounds with their small boats; many boats fitted with them can be seen at the Inlet, Atlantic City.

The mast should be steeped well up in the bow and should support a small sprit sail. Two lee-boards are used, although one would answer by shifting it over every time a tack was made. The board hangs over the leeward side and is about three feet long and ten inches wide at one end and fourteen at the other. The wide end hangs in the water and acts as a centre board, while it is supported at the narrow end by a rope. A small boat should be steered by an oar over the stern, as in riding the swells the stern and rudder are often out of water, when she is apt to fall away and capsize.

WINTERING.

As the days grow short and chilly a winter's berth for the yacht will have to be looked for. If it is the intention of the owner to keep her afloat all winter she should be drawn up into some quiet basin out of the influence of the tides and where she will be protected from the floating ice and heavy gales. Or she can be floated near to the shore on a spring tide, where she would be out of the water most of the time. Select an easy shore with a southerly exposure, as the heavy winter winds come from the northeast and northwest. A few days before the spring tides, which are higher than the usual tides, and which occur at the first and last quarter of the moon, preparation should be made for getting the yacht as high on the beach as possible.

On a bright, sunny day hoist the jib and mainsail and let them flap about in the breeze, with the peak of the mainsail hanging and the sheets loose. Bring out the light sails, topsail, squaresail and others, and spread them out in the sun so as to get perfectly dry, and in the middle of the afternoon, before the damp breezes of evening blow, roll up the light sails, unhook the sheets, downhauls and halliards from

the larger sails, and unlace them from the spars and stays.
Roll up all the sails securely and put them in a dry, well
ventilated loft. Occasionally on sunny days during the
winter they should be looked over and opened out to dry if
there are any signs of mildew, which if allowed to spread
would soon ruin an expensive sail. Never leave them in
the cabin of the yacht.

Next take up the flooring of the cabin and remove the
ballast, which is generally pigs of iron, sometimes made to
fit the curvature of the position of the hull in which they lie.
This, it is hardly necessary to say, should be removed in a
barrow or wagon to a place of safety. The centreboard
should be drawn up and securely fastened.

As she now floats very light she should at the highest
tide be brought as close to the shore as possible, the anchor
carried out on shore for some distance, a hole dug and one
of its flukes buried, securely anchoring the yacht to the
shore to prevent her from going adrift should she be floated
by a higher tide than usual. She will be comparatively
secure in this position, unless the ice is blown ashore during
high water.

A rope or chain should be attached to her stern and
fastened to a tree or post on shore. Her rudder had better
be unhung and placed in the cabin. Put two or three large
blocks of wood under her sides to keep her on an even keel,
or run ropes from the masthead to supports on shore. The
stays should be loosened, and they can be used for steady-

ing her by adding rope enough to make them sufficiently long. Knocking out two or three of the blocks or wedges between the mast and the deck will give the forehold ventilation. The ports in the side of the trunk should be left open slightly, which will ventilate the cabin.

Everything that can be injured by dampness should be removed from the cabin, as during the winter the moisture will condense and make her very damp inside, and for this reason she should be occasionally thrown open on clear days.

If you wish to secure her altogether from the danger of floating ice, get a rigger to put his crab or windlass near her and by putting greased planks on the sand and blocks under the yacht she may be drawn up clear of the water.

In the spring the mast should be scraped by using a boatswain's chair, which somewhat resembles a swing-board, to which the halliards is hooked. This had better be done by an experienced man. All moderate seams should be left as they are, but slightly caulk up very wide ones. Then rub down her hull with sand paper and pumice and give her two coats of paint.

After the paint is dry launch her at high tide, but do not anchor her very far from the shore as it is probable she will leak like a seive and go to the bottom. Keep her in three or four feet of water so that she can be pumped out at low tide. Let her soak for about a week, by that time her seams will have closed, and the water can be baled out, when she will be found as tight as a drum.

See that the centreboard works all right, as it is liable
to become wedged in the well by gravel or other foreign
substances. By uncovering the top of the well and running
a saw or stiff wire down alongside the centreboard it can be
cleaned without beaching the yacht.

The ballast should now be stowed so that the yacht will
be trimmed properly. If she was in proper condition the
previous summer no alteration is necessary, and the pigs
should be replaced in the same places from where they were
removed. As a general rule the ballast should be arranged
so that the stern is slightly deeper than the bows, from six
to eight inches probably, for a yacht twenty-five feet long,
although no special rule can be given for this and experience
alone must determine the proper trim for each yacht.

The mainsheet should be bound to the hoops then
fastened to the gaff, by attaching the throat and stretching the canvas along the gaff, and lashing the peak to
the end, then run the lacing. The boom is to be laced
in the same manner, using a small tackle if necessary, the
topping lift tackle for instance. Attach the jib to the forestay. Hook on the halliards, topping lift, sheets and other
running tackle. The stays should be set up after replac-
ing the wedges around the mast. Again the summer sets
in and you are now prepared for another season of sailing
and camping.

ELEVENTH ANNUAL REGATTA Q. C. Y. C.

The day of the eleventh annual regatta of the Quaker
City Yacht Club, Wednesday, June 9th, 1886, was ushered
in by an increasing cloudy atmosphere and a very moderate
breeze from the Southeast. By the time the large excursion
steamer chartered for the occasion, the Thomas Clyde, had
drawn up to the wharf adjoining the Quaker City Club House
the breeze had slightly freshened. The river was full of
pleasure craft, propelled both by wind and steam, and there
was great bustle along the wharves and on the water. Row
boats danced over the swell caused by the ferry boats from
yacht to shore and from shore to yacht, carrying the members
of the club bent on various errands in regard to the coming
event.

The yachts entered for the regatta, each having a large
black numeral or letter sewn on the peak of the main-sail,
were moored a short distance above the excursion boat. The
smallest, the Hurley, of the fifth class, and the only open
yacht entered this season, was about opposite the Thomas
Clyde, on which were the judges. The Hurley was anchored
well over toward the upper end of Ridgway Park, the various

yachts of the next class, the third (27 to 32 feet in length, there being no fourth class this season), were anchored on an approach to a diagonal line, that extended from the Hurley up the river toward the Camden shore, the first class sloops being at the upper end of this imaginary line. Still above them but nearer the middle of the river were the schooner yachts, the only schooners entered for several seasons past. They were the Helen and the Avalon. The others were: First class (cabin yachts 38 feet and over), the Venitzia, the winner in 1885, when she was first entered; the Minerva, which came in about twelve minutes behind the Venitzia in 1885, and the Sunbeam, which was thrown out of the 1885 regatta by the breaking of her mast in the Horseshoe. Second class (32 to 38 feet), Olga, a new sloop, and Consort. Third class, (27 to 32 feet), Agile, Carrie Z., Anita, Minerva and Nahma, the last three of Trenton. These made a fleet of thirteen handsome yachts, all with their mainsails hoisted, but the peaks hanging.

At 11 o'clock sharp the Clyde signalled with her steam whistle to get ready. The tugs and steamers which had been chartered by various clubs, and which were circling around before the line of contestants, drew to one side, the ferry boats delayed their trips for a few minutes, and at 11.05 the gun was fired.

Instantly the mainsail peaks pointed upward, the jibs slid up their stays, drawn by muscular arms, and in ten seconds the yachts were heading down the river, all except the

Agile on the port tack, the open yacht Hurley leading. Close after her was the Minerva, of Trenton, quite a favorite, with her projecting stern giving her the appearance of being only half supported by the water.

After the smaller yachts had passed, the Venitzia, large Minerva and Sunbeam came, and last of all the two schooners. In three minutes all had run up topsails and jib topsails and were dancing along to the dulcet strains of a brass band.

Just before reaching Gloucester it seemed to be a case of nip and tuck between the two schooners, both being on the port tack and close together, the Avalon to windward and, apparently, a trifle ahead. The Helen came about on the starboard tack, and, having the right of way, compelled the Avalon to put about to prevent being run into. This manoeuvre gave the Helen the wind when she slowly drew ahead of her rival. The Helen did not seem to sail as close to the wind as did the Avalon. It is a question whether she was unable to, or whether her captain found it the best policy to present more of a broadside to the wind, so as to make the sails draw better and thereby increase her speed. The steamers forged ahead, leaving these interesting schooners in the Horseshoe, and, passing the smaller craft, caught up with the first class sloops near lonely-looking Block Island, all the more desolate since the light house has been removed. Here the Venitzia was leading the Sunbeam. The distance between these two sloops at the head of the line was about as great as was the distance between the two schooners at the after end of the line.

Before the steamers reached the turning point, the upper Chester buoy, the Venitzia and Sunbeam had completed half a mile of their return voyage, the Venitzia about two hundred yards ahead. Just then a shout went up from the excursionists as the Venitzia's topsail and jib topsail doubled up and hung half way down the mast. The extreme top of her topmast had given away to the strain put upon it, as there was a rattling breeze at the time.

Now was the time for the Sunbeam to strain every stay, press forward and close up the gap. Out went the spinnaker boom, preparatory to running up that immense sail, but it was not time to spread it then, as the wind was on the starboard quarter, and to make use of that sail it would be necessary to have the wind further astern, and to put the yacht in such a position would have directed her course to the Pennsylvania or leeward side of the river, which would necessitate the taking in of the spinnaker, bringing the wind on the starboard beam and recrossing the river, thereby throwing her further behind instead making her gain on the disabled yacht. The two passed out of sight while the other yachts rounded the turning buoy.

The third to go around was the Nahma amid great excitement, and the Hurley was sixth, which was a very good position for an open boat, and that the smallest of the yachts, to maintain in a distance of sixteen miles with a strong breeze. Evidently the Agile lost time at the start by getting under way on the starboard tack, as she had to put about immediately afterwards, and by the time that was accomplished the breeze had decreased considerably, while further down where the rest were the breeze had not diminished.

The schooners Helen and Avalon passed respectively ten and twelve, about half a mile apart, the Carrie Z. being between them. The great spread of canvas and their superior size enabled the two schooners to pass all the others on the homeward trip, excepting the first class sloops, which had proven their superiority in sailing close-hauled.

Shortly after the schooners had rounded, the steamers caught up with them, thereby presenting to their passengers the beautiful sight of two schooners under a perfect cloud of canvas rushing through the water and throwing a mass of foam from their bows with the wind on the starboard quarter.

The handsome new schooner, the Avalon, had seven sails set viz: mainsail, foresail, jib, jib topsail, flying jib, maintopsail and maintop staysail, and all full. Unfortunately she was lightly ballasted and had almost too much sail for her stability as she heeled over considerably more than did the Helen, which sat almost upright, and which had one additional sail, the fore topsail. The jibs of the Avalon were larger than those of the Helen, and they seemed to press her head down. As her fore topsail was not shaken out to the breeze and as a pole maintopsail was run up, which gave her more sail aft, it is probable her captain did this to counteract some of the pressure on the head sails. Perhaps her head would have been higher had he taken in the flying jib. She was in an excellent condition for a light wind, but with the breeze she had, six or eight more tons of ballast would probably have made a very different ending to the race.

Putting on steam the large excursion boat slowly drew ahead of this grand sight to the tune of the Mikado Waltz, and the crowd of ladies and gentlemen, five hundred or more patronized the lunch counter, where sandwiches, pies, cider, soda and sarsaparilla were seized with avidity and eaten with a hearty appetite, caused by the excitement and the fresh breeze.

Catching up with the Venitzia and Sunbeam, the former still ahead with a drooping topsail, the latter just running out her spinnaker, as they were in the neighborhood of Gloucester, where the river bends and where the wind would be astern, the steamer kept their company for awhile. At the same time the Venitzia's spinnaker was run out, as her captain had made good use of the time since the carrying away to hitch a block near the top of what remained of the topmast. Through this block the spinnaker halliard was reeved, and the spinnaker, with the head doubled up in a bunch to allow for the difference in the length of the broken topmast, had been run up. The stay that supports the spinnaker boom, as it runs only to the masthead, was not affected by the break. In this fashion she came up first to the flag boat, at 2.37.40, amid the cheers of the crowd, the screams of the steamboat whistles and the band playing a mad gallop. She resembled a big white cumulus cloud dropped from the sky and blown across the surface of the water.

On account of the difference of size between her and the Sunbeam, which was pressing close behind, another big white cloud, it was necessary for her to get in fifty seven seconds ahead of the Sunbeam to win. It was three minutes later when the Sunbeam passed, took in her spinnaker and gracefully swung around the flag boat.

Then came the Helen and Avalon with the Minerva between, about the same distance apart as they were when below Gloucester. But, wonderful to behold, the Avalon had set an immense balloon jib, the other jibs having been taken in. A few more tons of ballast would have made her even with the Helen, without doubt.

The Nahma, the next boat, was the best in her class. The Consort, right after, the best in hers. Unfortunately the other yacht of this class, the Olga, also carried away her topsail. After the Consort came the Trenton Minerva.

With the last yachts came a few drops of rain and after cheers and whistle blowings the Thomas Clyde crossed the river and landed her passengers at Arch Street wharf, the band playing "Home Again." Every one feeling that with the cloudy day and good breeze, they had an enjoyable time in witnessing the most noble sport of America or of the world.

NAUTICAL TERMS.

The following is a short list of the terms most frequently used by yachtsmen, and are principally the ones used in the foregoing pages. When a word has two or more definitions, the one most applicable to the management of a sloop yacht is given.

AFT. Toward the stern.

AMIDSHIPS. The middle of the vessel, in regards either to her length or breadth.

ANCHOR. A heavy iron instrument for holding vessels, consisting of a straight shank having a ring for fastening the chain at one end, and curved arms at the other, ending in broad, flat flukes; a cross bar is attached below the ring at right angles with the flukes.

ASTERN. Behind the vessel; toward the after part.

BAILER. A scoop made of leather with a wooden handle.

BALLAST. Iron or lead placed along the keel to steady the vessel.

BALLOON JIB. A large jib extending from top of foretop mast to end of bowsprit or jib boom, thence to foremast.

BEAM. The width from side to side; the space between the bows and stern.

BELAY. To fasten a rope by twining it diagonally around a cleat.

BIGHT. The bend of a rope when it turns on itself; a loop.

BLOCK. Flat, generally oval, pieces of wood, protecting a sheave or pulley and used to change the direction of a rope or to increase the mechanical power.

BOATHOOK. A pole with an iron hook and straight prong at the end.

BOLT ROPE. Rope sewed around the edges of the sails to strengthen them.

BOOM. The long heavy spar to which the foot of fore and aft sails are attached.

BOW. The forward part of a vessel.

BOWSPRIT. The spar extending forward from the bows to which the forestay is attached.

BROACH TO. To fly up into the wind.

CABLE. A heavy rope for anchoring, made by twisting

61

three or four ordinary ropes.

CANVAS. General term for the sails.

CARVEL BUILT. The planks laid edge to edge.

CENTREBOARD. A heavy broad board that is let down through the bottom of a vessel to prevent her from making leeway.

CLEAT. Piece of wood or iron attached to the deck or spars for fastening ropes to.

CLINKER BUILT. The planks lapping.

CLOSE HAULED. Sailing as near as possible against the wind.

COUNTER. The curving part of stern.

CRINGLE. Loop of rope worked into the bolt rope of a sail, to assist in reefing.

CUTTER. A fast-sailing sloop-rigged vessel, with reducible bowsprit.

DECK. The upper flooring of the hull.

DOWN. To leeward.

EBB TIDE. The falling tide.

FLEET. A number of vessels keeping in company.

FLOOD TIDE. The rising tide.

FLOTILLA. Fleet of small vessels.

FLUKES. The broad plates on the arms of the anchor.

FORE. The foremost.

FORESAIL. The principal sail on a foremast; on cutters the sail set on the forestay.

FORWARD. In the direction of the bows.

FURL. To take in altogether and bind a sail to its spar.

GAFF. The spar that extends the tops of fore and aft sails.

GIG. A light, narrow boat.

GOING ABOUT. Tacking.

GOING FREE. With the wind on the beam.

GOING LARGE. Sailing with the wind on the quarter.

GROMMET. A ring of rope.

GUNWALE. The uppermost planking that finishes off the hull.

GYBING. The action of the wind when astern in swinging the boom over from one side of the yacht to the other.

HALLIARDS. Ropes used to hoist the sails.

HAWSER. A large rope ten inches in circumference or less; when of larger size it is designated a cable.

HELM. The tiller and its connections, the wheel, chain, etc.

HITCH. A species of knot.

HULL. The body of a vessel.

JAWS. The semicircular end of a gaff or boom.

JIB. Large triangular sail set on the fore stay in sloops and very useful in tacking.

JIB TOPSAIL. The sail next forward of the jib.

KEDGE. A small anchor.

KEEL. The heavy lowermost timber running the full length of the vessel to which the stem and stern posts are secured and also the ribs.

LARBOARD. Left side looking toward the bow; port.

LASHED. Bound with a rope.

LEAD. A conical weight used for sounding.

LEE. The side opposite to that from which the wind is blowing.

LEEBOARDS. Boards hanging over the leeward side of a small boat to reduce leeway.

LEECH. The aftermost part of a fore and aft sail.

LEEWAY. Drift sideways while sailing with wind on beam or bow.

LIFE LINES. Lines attached to the bottom of unballasted boats to which the crew hold on and lean backward when the wind is on the beam.

LUFF. To head more to the windward; the foremost part of a fore and aft sail.

LYING TO. Keeping the vessel's head steady under reduced sail so as to make little headway.

MAIN. Principal or largest.

MARLINE, Small line lightly twisted, used for bending sails, etc.

MAST. The heavy, upright timber supporting the spars and sails.

MIZZEN. Aftermost.

MOOR. Strictly speaking to secure by two anchors to prevent being swung by the tide.

MOORINGS. A chain attached to a block of stone or heavy anchors, permanently sunk, to which vessels make fast; the free end of chain is located by a buoy.

OAR. A long cylindrical piece of wood, one end expanding into a broad thin blade; for propelling small boats.

PAINTER. Rope attached to the bows of a boat for making her fast or towing.

PEAK. The upper, after end of a fore and aft sail.

PORT. Left hand side of a vessel looking forward; used in preference to larboard to prevent confusion and mistakes.

REEF. To reduce sail.

REEF PENNANT. Rope for securing after end of sail when reefed.

REEF POINTS. Small pieces of cordage fastened to the sail to diminish size, by tying around spar.

REEVE. To pass a rope through an aperature, as a block or deadeye.

RIGGING. The ropes of a vessel; running rigging for managing the sails, and standing rigging for staying the masts and spars.

RINGBOLT. An iron ring fastened to the deck by a bolt.

ROWLOCK. The attachment on the gunwale in which the oars work.

RUDDER. The flat timber attached to the sternpost by which the vessel's course is governed.

RUDDER POST. Post running through the counter to which the tiller is affixed.

RUN. Bottom of the yacht beneath the floor of the cockpit.

SADDLE. Block of wood attached to the mast to support the boom.

SCAG. The narrow part of stern forward of rudder.

SCHOONER. A fore and aft vessel having two or three masts.

SEA ANCHOR. Sails and spars tied together and thrown overboard to prevent drifting.

SERVE. To wind yarn around a rope.

SEIZE. To fasten two portions of a rope by lashing.

SHEET. Rope that is used in altering the position of a sail.

SLACK. Loose.

SLOOP. A fore and aft vessel with single mast and standing bowsprit.

SPAR. General term for mast, yard, boom, etc.

SPINNAKER. Large sail extended by a light boom on the side opposite to the mainsail while running before the wind.

SPRIT. A light spar attached to the mast by a beckot and extending the peak of the sail; used on small boats.

SPRITSAIL. A sail extended by a sprit.

SQUALL. A sudden transitory storm.

STARBOARD. To the right hand looking forward.

STAYS, Ropes used to steady the standing spars.

STEP. To set up a mast.

STERN. The after part of a vessel.

STORM TRYSAIL. Triangular sail lashed to the mast in place of the mainsail while scudding.

STRAKE. Plank running lengthwise in the side of a vessel.

TACK. To proceed against the wind.

TACKLE. A purchase by blocks and ropes.

TAUT. Tight. [boat.

TENDER. A yacht's small

THROAT. The portion of the gaff next the mast.

THWARTS. The seats extending across a rowboat.

TIDE. A periodical movement of the sea.

TILLER. The lever by which the rudder is turned.

TRIM. To set the sail or arrange the ballast to advantage.

TRUNK. The part of the cabin that extends above the deck.

TRUSS. A support for the boom while at anchor.

UP. To windward.

WEAR. To change direction of wind over the stern.

WEATHER. To windward.

WELL. The boxing which encloses the centreboard.

YACHT. Light, fast sailing vessel, used for pleasure or racing.

YAWL RIG. The rig of a sloop with a small mizzen mast.